ASPECTS OF GREEK LIFE

GREEK EXPLORATION AND SEAFARING

KENNETH McLEISH

LONGMAN

CONTENTS

1: The land and the sea

The Land of Greece

In the time of the Ancient Greeks (about 2000–250 BC) there was no country in the world actually *called* Greece. The Greek people (or **Hellenes**, as they called themselves) lived in hundreds of tiny, separate city-states, all over the area shown on the map.

The main reason for this separation was mountains. Look again at the map—each of the islands in the Aegean Sea is actually a mountain-peak standing out of the water, and three-quarters of the land surface is covered by hills over 1500 feet high.

The photograph shows the most famous of all Greek mountains. It is over 9500 feet high, and the Greeks believed that Zeus and the other gods lived on the summit.

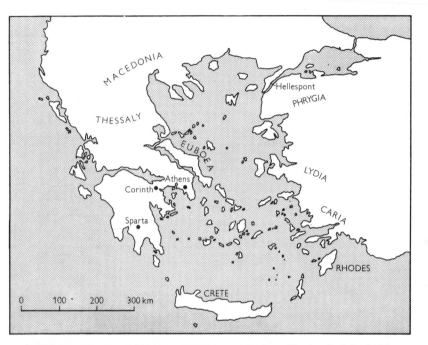

The land of the Hellenes

Mount Olympos

The top picture on this page shows how even the most fertile plains are hemmed in by mountains. There is hardly anywhere in Greece where you can walk for 25 kilometres without climbing at least one hill.

In countryside like this the best way to travel is not by road at all, but by sea. Few towns in Greece are out of sight or sound of the sea; everywhere there are natural harbours, inlets and magnificent bays like the one shown in the bottom picture.

Even today, with modern road surfaces, water-travel is as common as land-travel— and often far more comfortable. In Ancient Greece road-building methods were primitive, and the sea was often the only way of getting from one place to another.

Mountains near Sparta

The coast near Marathon

Colonies

But the sea was even more important to Greece than that. Without it many Greek states would not have survived at all.

The main reason for this was the poor quality of the soil. There is very little rainfall during the year: in summer the riverbeds dry up, and the countryside becomes barren and parched like the place shown in the picture.

The crops that grow best under these conditions are grapes and olives, and these were an important part of Ancient Greek agriculture. The soil was too poor to grow much corn, and the only farm-animal that did really well was the goat, which can eat almost anything and live almost anywhere.

A hilly landscape in northern Greece

As towns grew bigger, it very often happened that the soil was too poor to grow enough food for all the inhabitants. When this happened there was only one thing to do: to prevent everyone starving to death, some of the population had to move out. Boatloads of people would leave their native towns in Greece, and set sail to find new homes somewhere else. Sometimes they drowned, but very often they landed safely, and soon built up flourishing cities of their own.

On the opposite page is a map of the most important colonies founded by Greeks between 800 BC and 500 BC. Settlers from Greek city-states travelled to most parts of the known world, and built colonies wherever land was available, from the far west of Spain to the eastern shores of the Black Sea.

Greek Colonies (800–500 BC).

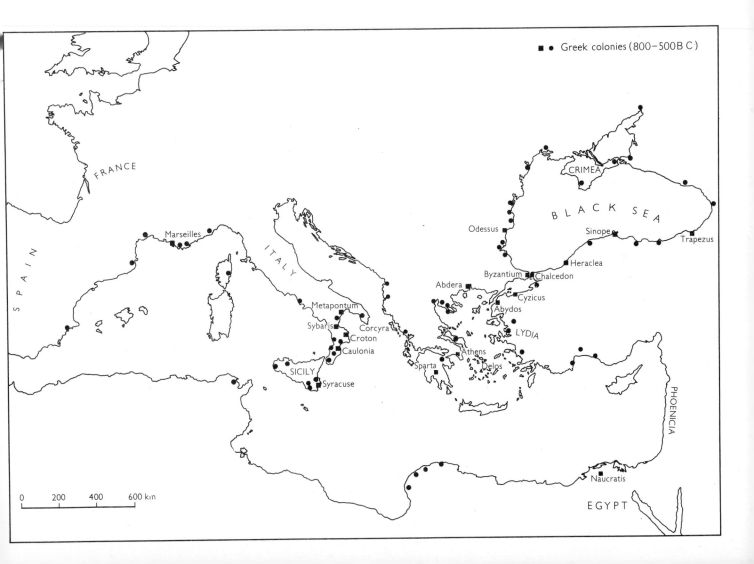

■ ● Greek colonies (800–500 B C)

FRANCE

SPAIN

ITALY

Marseilles

Metapontum

Sybaris
Corcyra
Croton
Caulonia

SICILY
Syracuse

Sparta
Athens
Delos

Abdera
Byzantium
Chalcedon
Cyzicus
Abydos
LYDIA

CRIMEA

BLACK SEA

Odessus
Heraclea
Sinope
Trapezus

PHOENICIA

Naucratis

EGYPT

0   200   400   600 km

From the map you can see that almost all of the colonies were on the coast, or very near it. The Greeks seldom went inland, even when the land was good. For 'mother-states' the sea was essential, both for founding colonies and for trading with them once they *were* founded.

Colonies usually kept up the links with their mother-states, and helped them in a number of ways. The most important were:

1. War. Colonies and their mother-states were allies, and would usually help each other in wartime. This was particularly useful if the colony happened to be near one of the enemy's main supply-routes.

2. Trade. Most colonies were in areas with fertile soil, or where there was a good supply of trade goods. Quite often a colony grew richer than its mother-state, and was able to send back corn or other goods to ease the shortage at home.

A Greek mother-state (Corinth) . . .

. . . and one of the areas she colonized (the Greek theatre at Syracuse in Sicily)

Poseidon, God of the sea

Because they realised that their country couldn't exist without the sea, and that 'Greece' was made up of as much salt water as dry land, the Greeks thought that Poseidon, the god of the sea, was second in power only to Zeus himself.

In the picture you can see a statue of Poseidon. It was discovered in the sea, and even though the eyes and the trident from its right hand are missing, it still gives the feeling of a magnificent and powerful god.

The Greeks believed that if Poseidon's trident fell on land it would cause an earthquake, but if it landed in the sea there would be a terrible storm.

Poseidon

There were temples and shrines of
Poseidon everywhere, and people prayed to
him before each voyage, and made
sacrifices of thanksgiving when they reached
their journey's end safely.

The finest temple of Poseidon that survives
today is at Sounion in Attika, nor far from
Athens. It is built on a headland, and—like
the 'white cliffs of Dover'—can be seen from
miles out at sea.

The picture on this page shows what it
looks like today. On page 13 you can see a
view from the temple looking out to sea.

Storms

Greek sailors knew nothing of the compass, and had almost no other aids to navigation. If they sailed at night—which was rarely—they used the stars for guidance. But usually they kept to the daytime, and avoided sailing altogether in winter. In the months when they did go to sea, they normally made short voyages of 50–100 kilometres, keeping land in sight as long as possible.

From the picture (which shows two merchant-ships) you can see how hard some Greek ships must have been to manage, especially in storms. With all that rigging, and sails that size, it might seem that the crew's chances of surviving a severe storm were very slight indeed.

Merchant-ships (from a vase-painting)

The Aegean and Mediterranean Seas are still famous for the suddenness and violence of their storms. Greek vase-painters often drew pictures of shipwrecks like the one on this page. The ship has turned completely upside-down, and the men are providing a meal for fish of all shapes and sizes.

In his play *Agamemnon* the poet Aischylos describes an Aegean storm like this:

Fire and water, those old enemies,
Made friends for once, and came to kill us.
The winds waited for darkness: rough winds
From Thrace that took our ships and smashed them
Hard into each other's flanks. Overhead
A mad shepherd battered his flock
With rain and hail; ship butted ship
Like leaping rams at play; the sky screamed.
Next morning the whole sea had flowered
With wrecks and bits of men.

REVISION

See if you can answer these questions without looking back. The pages mentioned in brackets will help if you need it.

1 What name did the Greeks give themselves? (page 3)
2 Why was Mount Olympos famous? (page 3)
3 Why was water-travel important to the Greeks? (page 4)
4 What is most of the Greek countryside like? (page 5)
5 Why did the Greeks found colonies? (page 6)
6 How did colonies help their 'mother-states'? (page 8)
7 Who was Poseidon? (page 9)
8 What was built on Cape Sounion? (page 10)

2: Trade

In the last chapter you saw that Greece is parched and dry, with few of the natural resources that make a country rich. But the Greeks founded colonies in the richest, most fertile parts of the world, and so were able to import whatever they needed.

Some Greek towns grew rich because they had many colonies, or founded them in very fertile areas. Corinth, for example, had links with many towns in Sicily and the south coast of Italy, and became one of the biggest importers and exporters in Greece.

Other places, like the island of Rhodes, used colonial trade in a different way. They became prosperous because they were on important trade-routes. (Rhodes, for example, was on the main corn-route between Greece and Egypt.) These towns had large harbours, ideal for resting in the middle of a long voyage; they were the meeting-place for traders from all over the world, and grew wealthy not because of what they did, but because they were there at all.

Corinth today

Rhodes, showing the harbour

On the next page is a map showing six of the most prosperous Greek 'mother-states', and the names of some of their colonies. You can see from the map that between them these six places controlled the trade of quite a large part of the world.

From their colonies—apart from corn, the most vital import of all—the Greeks imported raw materials like iron, copper, leather, clay and wool. Then they exported *back* to the colonies finished articles made from these raw materials.

In this way the skill and taste of Greek craftsmen travelled everywhere. Some objects made by Greeks will be described in this chapter, and you'll see how they can come from most unlikely places, like northern France or the south of Russia—places inhabited in these times by very primitive peoples.

A modern barley harvest in Turkey

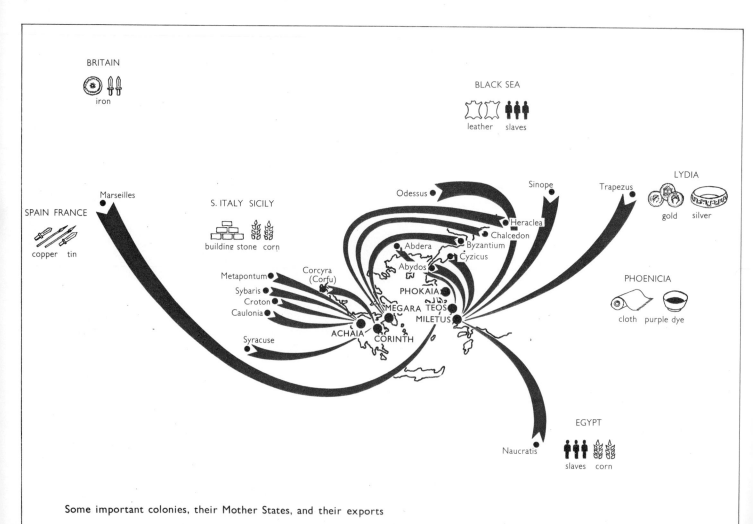

BRITAIN

iron

BLACK SEA

leather   slaves

LYDIA

gold   silver

Sinope

Trapezus

Odessus

Heraclea

Chalcedon

Byzantium

S. ITALY SICILY

building stone corn

Abdera

Cyzicus

Abydos

SPAIN FRANCE

copper   tin

Marseilles

Corcyra
(Corfu)

PHOKAIA

PHOENICIA

cloth purple dye

Metapontum

Sybaris

Croton

Caulonia

MEGARA TEOS

MILETUS

ACHAIA   CORINTH

Syracuse

EGYPT

Naucratis

slaves   corn

Some important colonies, their Mother States, and their exports

Coins

Coins were very important to colonial towns. Most colonies were in primitive areas, where money was unknown, and wealth was counted—very inconveniently—in sheep, cattle or even wives. By making and using its own coins, a Greek colony soon gained prestige, and established itself as the trading-centre of a whole area.

On this page and the next are photographs of colonial coins. They were made of bronze, gold or silver, and were as magnificent and impressive as possible. Some show the ruler or patron god of the town; others, like the coin in the lower left-hand picture on page 18 show the main export; but very many show objects from the sea, a reminder of how important the sea was to most colonies. All the coins on these pages are actual size.

Coin from Syracuse—
'heads'

The same coin—'tails'

Coin from the Crimea

The top three coins on this page show the patron gods of their cities:

1. Poseidon, from Poseidonia

2. the river-god Gelas, from Gela

3. Dionysos, from Naxos in Sicily

4. is from Metapontum in southern Italy, and shows an ear of corn. The towns in this area were rich farming communities, and exported corn all over Greece.

The other coins show their cities' connection with the sea:

5. is from Eretria, and shows an octopus

6. is from Akragas, and shows a crab.

1.

2.

3.

4.

5.

6.

Storage-jars: Amphoras

If an archaeologist of the future was turning over a 20th century rubbish-dump, the commonest objects he would find would be plastic or glass bottles, tins, and the remains of cardboard or wooden boxes. Thousands of these are used and thrown away, all over the world, every minute of every day.

The Greeks had disposable containers too, and thousands have been found on archaeological sites in Greece and the colonies. They are large earthenware jars called **amphoras**, with a very distinctive shape. You can see some in the pictures on this page and the next.

Amphoras were very easily stacked on their sides, and for this reason were widely used in ships, for carrying dry cargoes like corn and wet ones like wine or olive oil. The picture on this page shows the cargo from a Greek ship recently discovered by divers off the South Coast of France.

Amphoras on the sea-bottom

Corinth was the main centre of the Greek pottery trade, and over the years tens of thousands of amphoras must have been made there. The top picture, from a plaque in the temple of Poseidon near Corinth, shows amphoras being fired in a kiln. These are good-quality amphoras with carrying-handles —they would probably be used in the kitchen, not for ships' cargoes.

The middle picture shows an ordinary, simple amphora intended for everyday use. It is fairly plain—not like the amphora in the bottom picture. That one would have been extremely valuable even in Greek times. It was painted by the artist Exekias, and shows two Greek heroes, Ajax and Achilles, playing draughts.

Many of the pictures in this book are taken from ornamental Greek amphoras. Some of the finest artists worked in pottery, and their vase-paintings are not only beautiful, but tell us a great deal about ordinary life as well.

Amphoras in a kiln, from a plaque

Earthenware amphora

Amphora painted by Exekias

Trade goods

Some of the most popular of all trade goods were small articles made of **terracotta**. These were made from clay shaped in moulds, and then fired in an oven. They were small and cheap, very suitable for export. The most common type shows a god or goddess, or an ordinary person doing his everyday job.

The left-hand picture on this page shows a barber and his customer, and was made for export. You can see how easily it could be made from a mould—and it was once painted with natural colours, which have worn off in the course of time.

The right-hand picture shows a terracotta jug from Sicily. It is a standing figure, probably a goddess, and would be used for holding rose-water or oil.

You will find another terracotta group on page 30. This was perhaps intended to decorate a table, or stand on top of a box or chest. It is a domestic scene: two ladies are sitting on a sofa, gossiping.

Terracotta statuette

Terracotta jug

Terracottas were popular because they were cheap. But many ships carried expensive cargoes—articles made of gold, silver or bronze.

Sometimes bronze statuettes were made from moulds, just like terracottas. But more often the bronze articles carried would be household goods—expensive, luxury items, but still made for use rather than ornament.

On this page are photos of two things of this kind:

1. a **hydria** or water-jug, found near the trading-island of Rhodes

2. a mirror from Southern Italy. No glass was used—the bronze surface was highly polished and gave a clear reflection.

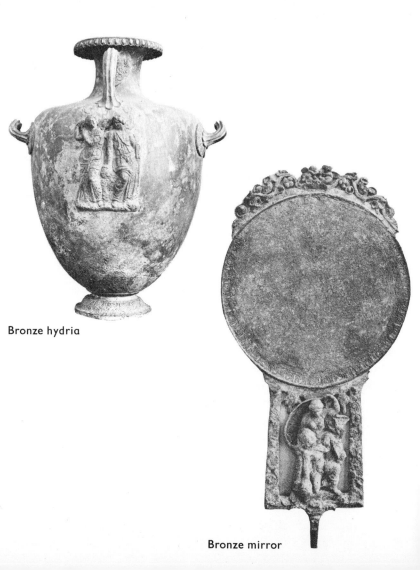

Bronze hydria

Bronze mirror

If you made a successful business deal, or were given good advice by a shrine or oracle, you would sometimes make the god a thank-offering of gold or silver. Small ferry-boats often carried worshippers from the mainland to one or other of the island shrines—like Apollo's on Delos or Aphrodite's on Cyprus—and some places collected so much treasure that they had serious security problems.

Sometimes the offerings were small, like the plaques in the bottom picture, which were found in Rhodes. But other offerings might be large and impressive, like the jug in the top picture. This was made from **electrum** (a mixture of gold and silver), and was found on an archaeological site in Central Russia.

Electrum jar

Gold plaques

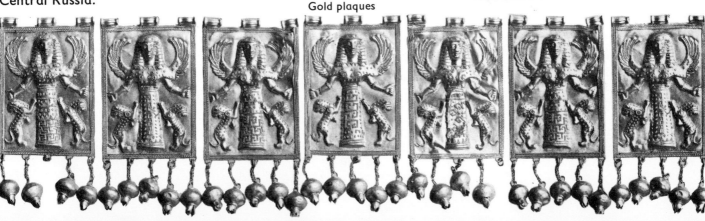

But perhaps the most beautiful and precious trade goods carried were articles of jewellery like those on this page. In the top picture you can see a gold bracelet. It is large and heavy, and would be worn on the upper part of the arm, just above the elbow.

The bottom right-hand picture shows a necklace. There is a ribbon of plaited gold thread, and a decorated clasp at each end. From it hang tiny golden amphoras—it's rather like a modern charm-bracelet, but meant for the neck instead of the wrist.

The bottom left-hand picture shows a pair of ear-rings. They are quite large, and must have been uncomfortable to wear for very long. They show Ganymede, the cup-bearer of the gods, being carried up to heaven by Zeus's eagle.

Gold bracelet

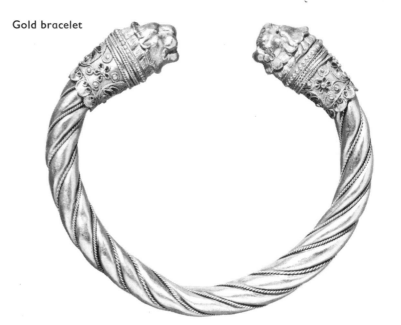

Gold ear-rings

Gold necklace

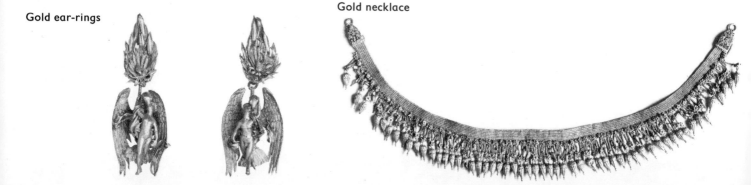

Insurance-and insurance frauds

With treasures like these on board, it's surprising that some Greek traders ever reached their destinations at all. Pirates lay in wait wherever the trading-vessels went, and insurance companies prospered.

The normal way of trading was this: you bought a ship, and borrowed money to buy a cargo. Then you insured this cargo and exported it to one of the colonies. There you sold it for a profit, and bought a new cargo to bring home. When this was sold—again for a profit—you repaid the original loan. So everyone was happy: the banker made 12% interest on his month's investment, and the ship-owner made a good profit out of his cargoes.

Some crooks made fortunes out of this system, by cheating everyone involved. There was a rule that if the ship was lost at sea— through storms, or because of pirates—the banker wasn't allowed to claim back his loan, and the ship-owner could also claim his insurance money. So, by faking a shipwreck, you might end up keeping the ship, with no loan to repay, and all the insurance money for the 'lost' ship and its cargo.

A merchant-ship being attacked by pirates (from a vase-painting)

Sometimes these schemes went wrong, and the crooks ended up in court. Here is part of the prosecution speech made at the trial of a crooked ship's-captain called Zenothemis:

Zenothemis was the captain of a ship owned by Hegestratos. They began by borrowing money in Syracuse, pretending that they needed it to buy a cargo of corn. But no corn was ever bought or loaded on to the ship. The arrangement with the bank was the usual one: if the ship arrived safely, the loan was to be repaid. But our crooks planned to sink it at sea, and so cheat both the bank *and* the insurance company.

So, one night, when they were two or three days' journey from land, on their way to Athens, Hegestratos went down into the hold and began cutting a hole in the bottom. Up on deck Zenothemis carried on as though nothing was happening. But a sudden noise warned everyone that something was going on in the hold, and they rushed down to see what it was. Hegestratos was caught red-handed; when he saw he was cornered, he jumped overboard to escape arrest. He meant to land in the dinghy, but missed because of the darkness, and was drowned. So he came to a richly-deserved bad end—the same, in fact, as he'd planned for everyone else.

A merchant-ship, with amphoras for corn or wine

His partner Zenothemis, left on board ship, at first exclaimed at the wickedness of the crime, as though he'd just heard of it. Then he tried to persuade the helmsman and the rest of the crew to take to the boats and leave the ship at once, as it was sinking fast with no hope of being saved. But they realised that this was just what he wanted—for the ship to sink and the bankers to be cheated. Their distrust of him was increased by the bankers' agent on board, who promised them a large reward if the ship was saved.

Through the efforts and bravery of the crew, and the help of the gods, the ship eventually reached Kephallenia. Zenothemis now pretended that it wasn't on its way to Athens at all, but had just come from there, and that he and the cargo were making for Marseilles, the home port of everyone concerned. But this didn't work either, as the authorities at Kephallenia knew very well that the ship was not only registered in Athens, but was on its way there on this occasion.

These crimes and lies would have been enough for any ordinary man; but Zenothemis wasn't finished yet. When the ship finally reached Athens, he had the nerve to claim that the non-existent corn was his own property, and had been all the time. He even took the bankers to court to prove it.

Zenothemis must have thought he was certain to win his case, simply because of the length of his journey—no one could easily check up on his story. He and Hegestratos were corn-traders, based in Athens, but sailing to and from Marseilles, with a halfway stop in Sicily—one of the longest and most dangerous trading-voyages possible.

With crooks like these to deal with, bankers and insurance companies took careful steps to make sure they *weren't* robbed: they put agents on board the ships, and kept pilots and guides stationed near dangerous parts of the coastline.

One very important step to protect corn-ships and their cargoes was taken in Alexandria in about 250 BC. On a small island in the river-mouth a lighthouse over 400 feet high was built. A fire was kept constantly alight at the top, and flashed for miles out to sea by means of bronze reflectors. The **Pharos** (as it was called, after the name of the island) stood for hundreds of years; it was regarded as one of the seven wonders of the world, and lighthouses like it were built by traders—and bankers!—in many parts of the world.

The *Pharos* of Alexandria (enlarged from a coin of about 185 AD).

REVISION

1 What was 'the most important import of all'? (page 15)

2 What sort of goods did colonies export? (page 16)

3 Why were coins important in primitive areas? (page 17)

4 What is an *amphora*? (page 19)

5 Name two things you could store in an amphora. (page 19)

6 What is *terracotta*? (page 21)

7 What gave the reflection in a Greek mirror? (page 22)

8 What were the main dangers for merchant-ships at sea? (pages 12, 25)

9 What is a *Pharos*? (page 28)

A merchant-ship being attacked by pirates from a vase-painting

THINGS TO DO

1 Make a model, in clay or plasticine, of an amphora, or of one of the terracotta or bronze figures on pages 21 and 22. You might like to make some jewellery, like the objects on page 24—or perhaps the statuette on this page will give you the idea for a scene from everyday life.

2 Visit a nearby museum and see what archaeological finds have been made near your own home town. Has the museum any Greek remains? What sort of things does it chiefly contain? Does it give you a good idea of how people used to live in the past?

3 Imagine you are Zenothemis. Write a speech in your own defence, explaining what *really* happened.

Gossips

3: Ships

Some of the earliest Greek ships we know about belonged to the Minoans of Crete. They ruled over a great sea-empire, and their pottery and stone-carvings are covered with pictures of ships and objects from the sea.

On this page are drawings taken from three Minoan seals. The top one was made in about 2000 BC, and shows an early boat, perhaps made of reeds lashed together.

The other two were made in about 1600 BC The bottom right-hand one shows quite a large ship for that time—only warships would have more oars than this. The bottom left-hand picture explains itself.

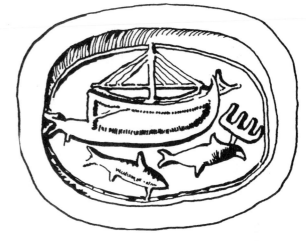

Sailing-ship

Galley with 36 oars

Sailor and sea-monster

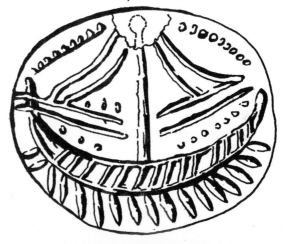

Here is a description, from Homer's *Odyssey*, of the building of a simple boat. Odysseus has been trapped on the island of the Nymph Kalypso; now the gods say it's time for him to leave.

Odysseus set to work at once. He felled 20 trees, rough-trimmed them with the axe, then smoothed them down till they were straight and true. Then Kalypso brought him drills, and he bored holes in the timbers and fitted them together, fastening them with clamps and wooden pegs. He made a keel as wide as a broad-bottomed merchant-ship, and fitted platforms to it at bows and stern, fastened to stout ribs. The whole job was finished off with planking down the sides, and a superstructure of woven wickerwork to protect him from the sea.

Next he placed in position the mast and its yard-arm, and a steering-oar to control the boat. On the bottom he piled logs for ballast. Then, with cloth supplied by Kalypso, he made a sail, and lashed it skilfully in position with the usual braces, sheets and halyards. When everything was ready and the boat was finished, he dragged it down on rollers into the calm sea.

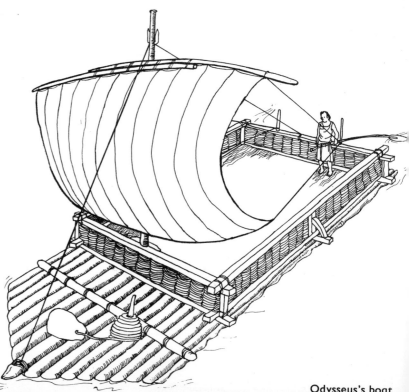

Odysseus's boat

Odysseus's boat was probably a raft, like Thor Heyerdahl's raft *Kon-Tiki*. He sailed quite safely in it for 18 days, and so escaped from Kalypso's island.

In those days, just as now, the launching of a ship was quite an occasion. Here is how Jason and his crew launched the *Argo*, ready to go and find the Golden Fleece:

They fastened ropes securely round the hull, pulling them tight on each side, so that the planks would cling to the bolts, whatever the force of the water. Next they dug a trench the width of the ship right down from the bows into the sea. The further they went the deeper they dug, placing polished rollers at the bottom of the trench, so that *Argo* could glide smoothly and easily down them into the water.

Up above, sticking out 50 cm on each side, they fastened oars across the whole width of the ship. Then the whole crew took up their positions, hands and chests on the oars, ready to heave as soon as the word was given. The helmsman gave a loud cry, and they heaved forward with all their strength, and started *Argo* moving. She began going faster and faster; the rollers creaked and groaned as they took the strain, and black smoke rose up as the timbers rubbed together.

At last *Argo* reached the sea, and they hauled her inshore and moored her. Then they fitted the oars in the proper positions, put up the mast, and loaded the sails and all the provisions for the voyage.

Pirates

From simple beginnings Greek ship-building progressed very quickly. The galley shown in the top picture is from a vase-painting. It's a very fine ship, with sleek, fast lines, and a powerful 'beak' at the front for ramming the enemy.

On page 25 there is a picture of a merchant-ship being attacked by pirates. The bottom picture on this page is from the same vase, and shows the pirate-ship in more detail. Notice the single sail, very simply rigged to a central mast, and the steering-oar at the back. One of the pirates is taking in sail, and the rowers have pulled in their oars, ready for the crash. Once their beak ripped a hole below the waterline, the merchant-ship would be easy prey.

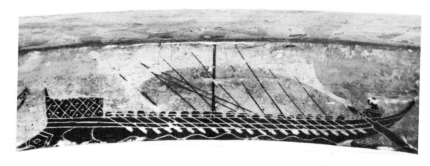

Greek war-galley

Pirate ship

Merchant-ships

Merchant-ships were broader and deeper than the fighting-ships on page 34; but in other ways they were made to the same design. There was one mast, usually with a huge single sail, and between 20 and 40 oars on a ship of average size. The steering was done with a long, broad-bladed oar controlled by a single helmsman on a high platform in the stern. On very big ships two steering-oars were needed, one at each side.

The picture on this page shows a 22-oared galley. It was in small ships like this that most trading-voyages were made. The helmsman (on the left) is not drawn to scale, of course: if he was, he'd be about 5 metres tall.

The largest Greek merchant-ship we know about was an Alexandrian corn-carrier, the *Alexandreia*. It was rated at 3,310 tons. But the usual tonnage was incredibly small: 50 tons, the same as a small coaster or large yacht nowadays.

22-oared trading-galley

Warships

The most famous of early Greek warships were called **penteconters**, which means '50-oared boats'. There were 24 rowers on each side, and 2 steering-oars. Their main trouble (as you can read on page 58) was that they couldn't turn or stop very easily. Going in a straight line and ramming the enemy head-on was what they could do best.

When Greek admirals realised how awkward penteconters were, they quickly found a way of streamlining them. In a penteconter the rowers all sit on the same level; by having *more* than one 'bank' of oars, you can get the same number of men into much less space. The diagram on the opposite page shows how it was done.

Several schemes were tried: **quinqueremes** (5 banks of oars, one above the other); **quadriremes** (4 banks); **triremes** (3 banks); **biremes** (2 banks).

Of all these the *trireme* turned out to be most useful, and soon became the standard type of Greek warship. The usual number of oars was 172—2 steering-oars and 170 rowers. This must have been very fast and efficient.

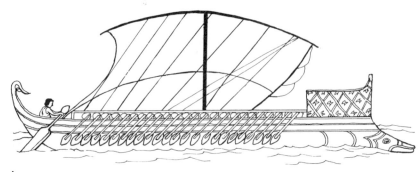

A penteconter

A trireme

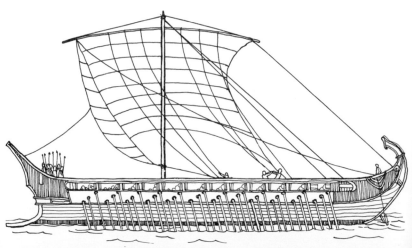

The diagram on this page, and the picture on page 36, show how the oars were arranged, seen from the side. The rowers sat in groups of three; there was a gap of I metre between each man and the next, and the lowest bank of oars was only 50 cm above the waterline.

A trireme had 25 under-officers, and 5 superior officers. The under-officers' main job was to keep the rowers working together; if there hadn't been a steady rhythm, the result would have been chaos. (It was rather like a cox and his crew in a modern racing-boat.)

Sometimes there were soldiers on board triremes too; but they never rowed, and the rowers never fought—the two jobs were always kept separate.

The picture on the next page shows a cut-away model of a trireme, and you can see from it that all three banks of rowers could work in fair comfort.

Oar-pattern of a trireme

The crew of a trireme was large, and the rowers must have been both skilful and highly-trained. Triremes were fast, efficient, and practically unbeatable in sea-battles.

Of course, you would expect naval warships to be fast, and their crews efficient. But ordinary seamen were just as highly skilled. Here is a description by Homer of a well-trained crew in action:

The crew, who knew their job well, took their places on the rowing-benches, and unfastened the mooring-rope from its pierced stone. Then, putting their backs into the work, they began to churn the sea to foam with their oars. Just as a team of four stallions, responsive to the whip, gallops eagerly across the plain, heads tossing and feet flying—just so did the ship rear proudly from the dark water that ran and bubbled away astern. On she sped, so light and fast that not even a wheeling hawk, the fastest thing that flies, could have kept pace with her.

Model of part of a trireme seen from above

REVISION

1 Where did the *Minoans* live? (page 31)
2 Look at the maps on pages 3 and 7. Why is Crete a good centre for
  a sea-empire? (page 14, last paragraph, may give you a clue)
3 What did Jason's men go to find? (page 33)
4 How did pirate-ships cripple their victims? (page 34)
5 How were Greek ships steered? (page 36)
6 What was a *penteconter*? (page 36)
7 How many men rowed in a *trireme*? (page 36)
8 Does the picture on this page show a *trireme*, a merchant-ship
  or a *penteconter*? (page 37)

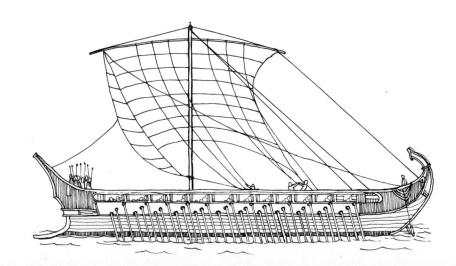

4: Tall Stories

Almost all towns of any size in Greece owned ships. When Homer, in the *Iliad*, mentions all the places that sent ships and men to the Trojan War, the list takes up over 300 lines of the poem, and mentions over 100 towns by name. Very few people in Greece *can't* have been interested in the sea.

This is perhaps the reason why so many Greek stories and legends are about seafaring. Descriptions of storms, battles and fantastic voyages are common—and so are stories of sea-monsters and supernatural events.

In this chapter are some 'tall stories' about the sea. The first is from *The Argonauts* by Apollonios (a book about Jason and the Golden Fleece), and the rest come from Homer's *Odyssey*, which is about Odysseus's adventures on his 10-year journey home from the Trojan War.

Coin from Ios showing Homer.

As you will see, some of the things described have no natural explanation at all; they're just good stories, the sort of tales sailors often tell. But others may well be based on real life, things we can still meet and see today.

On the next page, for example, is Apollonios's account of how *Argo* escaped from the Clashing Rocks. These were in the Bosphorus, at the narrow entrance to the Black Sea—a place still famous for its hidden rocks and dangerous currents.

We can't of course say what it was that made the Clashing Rocks *move*. Perhaps they were floating icebergs, or great boulders rolling down the cliff-face after an earthquake. But obviously a natural explanation is possible—perhaps you'll think of one yourself as you read Apollonios's description.

A story-teller

When they reached the narrow, winding straits, walled in by cliffs, they felt the current swirling against them, and were filled with a great fear. Their ears rang with the grinding and crashing of the Rocks, and the endless roar of water against the cliffs. They rounded a bend, and saw the Rocks opening ahead of them. Their hearts sank, but there was no choice but to go on, straight for the gap between the Rocks.

Suddenly the Rocks rushed at one another, and met with a thunderous crash. A storm of foam and white spray leaped up, and the sea groaned and thundered till the sky echoed. *Argo* was snatched by the current and whirled round in a helpless circle.

Then without warning the Rocks parted again, and the captain ran down the gangway between the rowing-benches, shouting to his crew to row as hard as they could. Eagerly they obeyed him, but the current was still too strong. Their oars bent like bows, but they were swept back three yards for every two they travelled.

Then another huge wave rushed down on them, and *Argo* rolled end-on and plunged through the rolling water. She was washed back between the Clashing Rocks, and wedged there unable to move. The current ebbed and flowed, and the Rocks rumbled and roared on either side, but *Argo* was stuck fast.

That was when Athene came down and took a hand. She thrust the solid rock aside, freed *Argo* and sent her speeding through the channel. On the ship flew, winged like an arrow—but even so, as the Rocks crashed shut, they snapped off the very tip of the superstructure at the stern. Apart from that, they were safely through—and Athene soared back up to heaven, her task complete.

Odysseus didn't have to pass through the Clashing Rocks on his way home from Troy. But he did have other problems to deal with—Polyphemos, for example, a one-eyed Sicilian giant who wanted to eat Odysseus and his men alive. But they tricked him in the end—first they blinded him with a heated pole, and then they escaped from his cave by clinging under the bellies of his sheep. The picture on this page shows the moment of blinding.

Then there were Scylla and Charybdis, sea-monsters who lived along a narrow sea-passage between tall cliffs. Scylla's lair was a cave high on the cliff-face. She had 12 feet, and 6 heads on scaly necks. When a ship passed through the channel, she darted her necks out of the cave, snatched a man in each pair of jaws and swallowed him alive. Charybdis lived a little further on, on the sea-bed. Three times a day she opened her huge mouth and gulped down the sea. Any sailors who escaped Scylla were certain to be sucked down by Charybdis.

Odysseus and Polyphemos

Nowadays people think that, when he wrote about Scylla and Charybdis, Homer was really describing the Straits of Messina, the narrow channel between Italy and Sicily. The currents there are fast and treacherous, full of whirlpools (Charybdis?), and rocks rumble down the cliffs and knock unwary sailors into the sea (Scylla?). It's still a dangerous place, even without Scylla's 12 legs and Charybdis's bottomless throat.

And as for Polyphemos—the simplest explanation of one-eyed flesh-eating monsters is that Odysseus and his men landed among ordinary cannibals, with an extra eye painted in the middle of their foreheads. Frightened men would remember them as giants, and from a distance it would seem as though they only had one eye.

Polyphemos, Scylla and Charybdis *can* be explained, if you want to. But it's not so easy to find a natural explanation for Circe, the witch who kept Odysseus and his men prisoners, and gave them a magic drug that turned all the crew into helpless, grunting pigs. (Odysseus himself only escaped because one of the gods had warned him in advance, and given him a different drug to stop the effects of Circe's poison.)

The picture on this page (from a vase drawn by a not-too-brilliant artist) shows Odysseus's horrified reaction as Circe offers him her drug. The strange object on the right is Circe's loom.

Odysseus and Circe

Some more female monsters, even worse than Circe, were the Sirens. Homer says that they were sea-nymphs, whose beautiful singing drew men on till they were wrecked on a jagged rock. Odysseus plugged his men's ears with wax, and they rowed safely on without hearing anything. But he himself wanted to hear the song, so he was tied to the mast, and so enjoyed the beautiful singing without coming to any harm.

In the picture you can see Odysseus and the Sirens. Some people say that what Odysseus *really* heard was the singing of a rare animal called the **dugong** or sea-cow. But meeting a herd of sea-cows wouldn't have made a very good story—the Sirens in the picture are much more interesting.

Odysseus and the Sirens

Perhaps it's a mistake to try and explain a good story. And the *Odyssey* is a very good one indeed, as you may agree when you read Homer's own descriptions of the monsters mentioned in this chapter. Most people just enjoyed tales like these without worrying whether the monsters actually existed or not. There were enough real dangers on the sea, without bothering about imaginary ones as well. What with storms, sunken rocks and pirates, quite a few Greeks must have agreed, in their heart of hearts, with Hesiod. He felt uneasy on the sea, and preferred the quiet life of a farmer. This is the advice he gives seafaring men:

If sea-travel, however uncomfortable, is in your blood and you can't give it up, learn weather-sense instead. At the end of the autumn, when the Pleiades run from the cruel Orion and plunge into the misty sea, gales and winds of all kinds will be raging. That's the time to keep off the wine-dark sea, and work the land instead. Haul your vessel up on shore, and pack stones all round it, to keep it safe from rain-soaked winds. Pull out the bung, or rain will rot the timbers. Take all the tackle and fittings indoors. Fold the sails (the wings of your swift ship) and store them carefully. Hang the well-made steering-oar over the fireplace, and wait for a better season for sailing.

REVISION

1 Who wrote the *Odyssey*? (page 40)
2 Whose story is told in the *Argonauts*? (page 40)
3 Where (and what) are the Clashing Rocks?
   (page 41)
4 Who was Polyphemos? (page 43)
5 How did Odysseus deal with him? (page 43)
6 What did Circe do to Odysseus's men? (page 45)
7 How did Odysseus escape the same fate? (page 45)
8 How did Odysseus's men escape from the Sirens?
   (page 46)

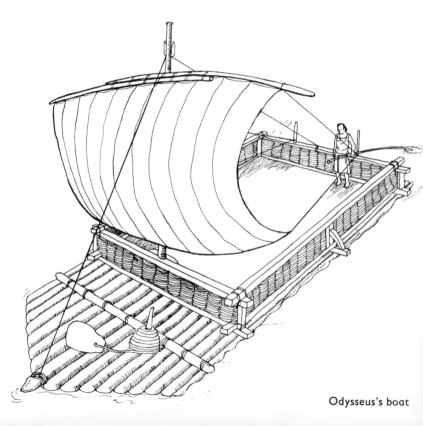

Odysseus's boat

THINGS TO DO

1 Find out more about Jason or Odysseus. (A booklist is given on page 63).

2 Make a model or drawing of a Greek ship. The pirate-ship on pages 25 and 34 would be a good one to choose, and Chapter 3 will give you all the details you need.

3 Imagine you are a Greek sailor, and write an account of one of your voyages, mentioning some of the dangers you had to face. The vase-picture on this page might suggest one scene to you.

5: Triumph and Disaster

In 480 BC the Greeks, led by Athens, totally destroyed a huge invading fleet from Persia. From that moment of triumph for the next 65 years, Athens was the leading state in Greece. Very many of the Greeks' greatest achievements—in poetry, science, philosophy, politics and the arts—date from this time, and the Athenians tried to make their city the richest and most beautiful in the whole of Greece.

Then, in 415 BC, an Athenian fleet set sail for Sicily to fight there. The Athenians expected an easy victory over their enemies, but instead their whole fleet was destroyed in a disastrous battle in the Great Harbour at Syracuse. Athens never really recovered from this crushing blow. Her ships had made her the leading state in Greece, and their defeat now ended her leadership for ever.

This chapter is about the two great battles: **Salamis**, Athens's moment of triumph, and **Syracuse**, her moment of disaster.

The Parthenon in Athens, her most famous building, built at the peak of her glory

Salamis

The story of Salamis begins in **485** BC, when
Xerxes became king of Persia. His father,
Dareios the Great, had been beaten by the
Greeks 5 years before, and Xerxes was
determined to avenge him. So he began
collecting an army, and making preparations
for the invasion that would destroy the
Greeks and make them his slaves for ever.

There were probably **800** ships in Xerxes's
navy, and **200,000** men in his army. But the
Greeks were used to armies of only **10,000**
men, and fleets of **80** or **90** ships. They were
terrified. Rumours flew about that thousands
of warships were coming, backed by more
than $2\frac{1}{2}$ million soldiers. Hastily they began
building a fleet of their own—paid for out of
the profits from a silver-mine recently
discovered near Athens.

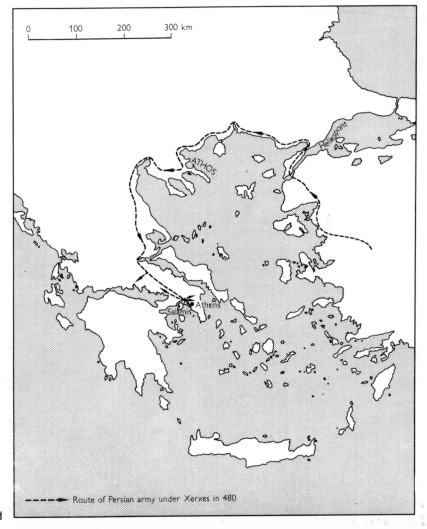

Xerxes's route westward

- - - - ► Route of Persian army under Xerxes in 480

Xerxes began by ordering his men to build
a bridge over the Hellespont. They did; but
the currents and strong winds smashed it to
pieces before it was finished. Xerxes was
furious, and ordered that the sea should be
given 300 lashes, and have chains thrown into
it, to show who was master. The unfortunate
bridge-builders were executed on the spot.

The new bridge-builders had a better idea:
they built *two* bridges, made of boats lashed
together. One used 360 penteconters, the
other 314. The picture shows how each
bridge was made. When the penteconters
were anchored and lashed together, wooden
planks were laid over them, and covered with
earth to form a roadway. They even built
fences so that the horses wouldn't see the
water and panic.

The bridge of boats

Xerxes and his men crossed the Hellespont, and marched to Mount Athos. Here Xerxes simply ordered his men to dig a canal all the way across. (This was probably near the bottom of the photo; remains of a channel have been found there, as well as 300 Persian coins.)

After this it seemed that nothing could stop Xerxes. He found a way through trackless mountains; his soldiers discovered food and water where none had been found before; no one could stand in his way. He even destroyed an army of Spartans, the greatest soldiers in Greece, who resisted him bravely but hopelessly in the narrow pass at Thermopylae.

As he came ever nearer, the Athenians grew more and more terrified. Then Themistokles, the man who had ordered the building of the fleet, took charge. He moved all the women and children out of the city, and—after a lot of arguing—persuaded the Greek army to take up a position on the island of Salamis, and the fleet to wait there for the enemy's arrival. You can see a map of the area on page 55, and a photo of it on page 54.

The peninsula of Athos

The Persian army easily captured Athens—there was no one left to defend it. Then they marched triumphantly down to Salamis, expecting to destroy the Greeks without any difficulty there as well. The fleet gathered round its prey, and Xerxes and his soldiers sat on the bank to watch the battle. (Xerxes even kept a notebook handy, ready to jot down the names of people he thought were fighting particularly bravely.)

The photo on this page shows the narrow straits where the Greek and Persian ships faced each other. It was taken from the spot where Xerxes probably sat. The diagram on page 55 shows how the Persians hemmed the Greeks in, with no hope of escape. As the Greeks were outnumbered by about four to one, it looked as though they had no chance.

The straits of Salamis

But they won all the same. Their ships were lighter and faster than the Persians', and could turn round and get away more easily. They were better trained, too, and had a plan of action, while the Persians fought blindly, hampered by the size and number of their ships.

Gradually the Greeks drove them into a tight knot in the middle of the straits. The Persians' oars and rigging grew hopelessly entangled, and because their ships were so big they couldn't free themselves or turn round and escape. Their oars were smashed, and the sides of their ships began creaking and groaning with the strain.

Still the Greeks pressed on, ramming ship against ship. Penteconter after penteconter capsized; the water was choked with wreckage, and the exhausted Persians floundered in the shallows among the corpses, while the Greeks finished them off one by one like stranded fish. Xerxes and the army fled.

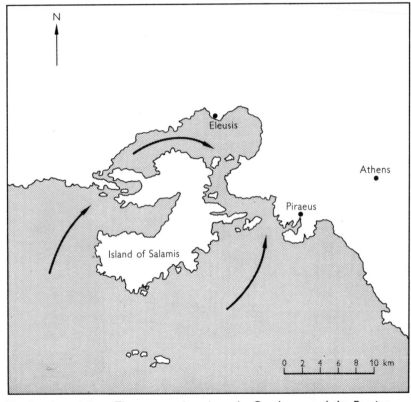

The battle positions. The arrows show how the Greeks penned the Persian ships into the narrowest part of the straits

Syracuse

After this success, the Athenians soon
became the leaders of Greece. And after
the Persians were driven back, no other
foreigners invaded Greece for nearly 300
years, until the Romans finally conquered her
in 136 BC.

But the Athenians were not popular
leaders. Other Greek states were jealous of
their success, and angry at their boasting.
The important trading-centre Corinth, and
the leading military state Sparta, had always
been rivals of Athens, and now began
collecting allies for a great war against her.
This war was finally declared in 431 BC.

Athens's soldiers did quite well in this war,
but never as well as her fleet, which was
always victorious. Then, in 415 BC, the
Athenians thought that the chance had come
to win or lose once and for all—and by using
ships. The enemy were gathering in Sicily,
particularly round Syracuse, the capital city,
which had a fine harbour. The Athenians
decided to send out the greatest fleet the
world had ever seen, and prove to the rest of
Greece that they were still the greatest and
strongest nation in the world.

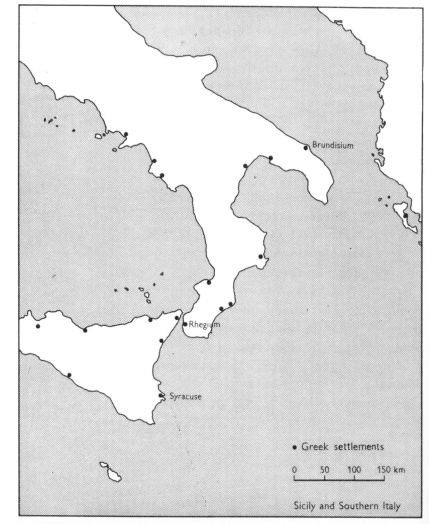

Brundisium

Rhegium

Syracuse

• Greek settlements

0   50   100   150 km

Sicily and Southern Italy

Here is an eye-witness's description of the fleet leaving Athens, by the historian Thukydides:

No expedition so costly or magnificent had ever before sailed from a single city. Both the State and individual ship-owners had spent lavishly: the public treasury provided each sailor with a drachma[1] a day, and supplied 100 empty ships, 60 to be fitted out as fighting-vessels, and the rest as troop-carriers. The ship-owners manned these vessels with the best crews available, and provided figure-heads and other equipment of the most expensive type. Each owner was anxious that his ship should be the fastest and best equipped in the whole fleet.

When all the equipment was loaded, and the crews were in position, a trumpet blew for silence, and the usual prayers were offered up. Wine was poured into the mixing-bowls, and on each ship the officers and crew made offerings to the gods from gold and silver cups, while everyone on shore joined in with prayers and offerings.

A warship, fully equipped and ready for action, carved in ivory

[1] 1 drachma = 6 obols. You could buy a loaf of bread for one obol.

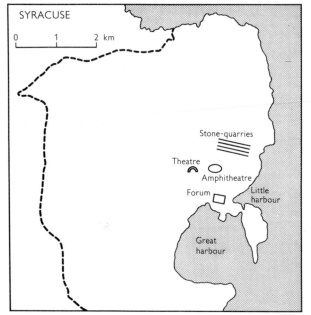

The Great Harbour at Syracuse

While the Athenians collected their forces at Corcyra (modern Corfu), the Sicilians quietly went on with *their* preparations in the Great Harbour at Syracuse:

Remembering what they had learned in earlier sea-fights, they began making improvements in their ships. In particular, they shortened and strengthened the prows, knowing that the Athenian ships would not be adapted in the same way. The battle was to be fought in the Great Harbour, where the ships would be crowded together; and the Syracusans hoped that their new tactics would bring them victory. They planned to charge prow-to-prow, and use their strengthened rams to smash in the enemy's bows, which were too flimsy and unprotected to withstand such thick, solid timbers. The Athenians would be trapped by the narrowness of the harbour, unable either to sail round them or move out of the way, the two manoeuvres they knew best.

This battle-plan turned Syracusan weakness into strength. Ramming prow-to-prow was a movement they were good at, and could use again and again. They thought that once the Athenians began to get the worst of it, they would bunch together in the narrow space, and so run foul of each other. And in fact that's just what did happen: the Athenians were bunched together and unable to escape, while the Syracusans, who controlled both the land round the harbour and the open sea, could draw back and make new charges, again and again, from whatever direction they wanted.

When it came to the battle, the Sicilians won a great victory—partly because of their preparations and partly because the Athenians were too sure of themselves. Here is Thukydides's account of the battle:

The Syracusans divided their fleet: some were sent to guard the harbour-entrance, and the rest were stationed all round it in a circle, so that they could attack the Athenians from all sides at once. They positioned their land-forces as a second line of attack, in case any Athenians reached the shore.

The Athenians sailed up to the harbour-mouth, and by force of numbers broke through the line of ships barring their way. But once they were inside the harbour the whole Syracusan fleet attacked them from all sides at once. No battle was ever greater or fiercer. The sailors on both sides were as eager to row hard against the enemy as the steersmen were to outdo each other in skill and alertness.

The two fleets together came to nearly 200 ships. They were jammed so tightly together in the narrow harbour that there was no opportunity for ramming or breaking back for a charge. There were frequent collisions, ship fouling ship as they attacked or fell back from one another. While two ships bore down on each other, the soldiers on deck showered their opponents with spears, stones and arrows. When they met, there was fierce hand-to-hand fighting as each crew tried to board the other ship.

Often, because of the cramped space, a man had no sooner killed his enemy than he was struck down himself; on several occasions two or more ships attacked the same enemy, and became entangled; steersmen frequently had to avoid several enemy ships at once. The crashing and splintering of ship against ship caused great confusion, and made it impossible to hear the orders shouted by the officers.

At last, after many hours' fighting, the Syracusans did succeed in routing the Athenian fleet, and with eager shouts of excitement and encouragement drove them back to the shore. Many of the sailors had been killed at sea; the survivors rushed ashore in panic, and the Athenian ground-troops, with one concerted groan of despair, turned and ran as well. Some hurried to defend the ships, or guard what was left of their camp, but the majority were only anxious to save their own skins.

The battle had been long and hard, and many ships and men had been lost on both sides. The victorious Syracusans gathered up the bodies of the dead, and salvaged what they could of the wreckage; then they sailed back to the city and put up a trophy. The Athenians were so crushed by the disaster that they never even thought of asking permission to gather up their dead or salvage their wrecked fleet. Their one thought was to wait for night, and then run for their lives.

This sea-battle shows the great drawback of using galleys as fighting-ships: they are quite useless in a narrow space, and very dangerous because of all the oars, and the large number of rowers exposed to attack.

But galleys remained the normal kind of fighting-ship right up to the 15th century when a new system of sails was invented that made it possible for large warships to move quickly without using oars at all.

The only major advance in sea-fighting in the 1000 years after Syracuse was the invention of 'Greek fire' in about 625 AD, by the engineer Kallinikos. He mixed saltpetre with the crude oil that welled up from the ground in many parts of the Greek empire. The explosive mixture was packed into amphoras; fuses were lit, and the amphoras were catapulted at the enemy ships. The results of this were spectacular, far better than just rowing hard at your enemy and ramming him below the water-line. If the Athenians had had Greek fire at Syracuse, the whole history of Greece would have been completely different.

This carving of a trireme in action gives a good idea of how vulnerable all the rowers would be in a cramped space

REVISION

1 Who was the king of Persia who was beaten by
the Greeks at Salamis? (page 51)
2 How did the Greeks finance their fleet? (page 51)
3 How did Xerxes cross the Hellespont? (page 52)
4 How did he cross the peninsula of Mount Athos?
(page 53)
5 Why were the Greek ships better than the
Persians' at Salamis? (page 55)
6 How did the Sicilians prepare their ships for the
sea-battle at Syracuse? (page 58)
7 What is 'Greek Fire', and how is it used? (page 61)

Greek
soldier

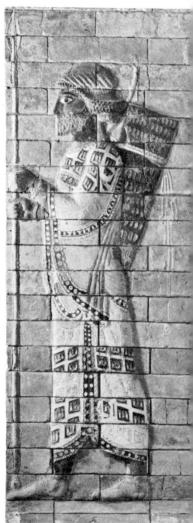

Persian
soldier

THINGS TO DO

1 Read some more about the Persian invasion of Greece, and chart its progress on a map. The booklist on this page, and the maps on pages 3, 51 and 55 will help.

2 Draw a picture showing the battle in the harbour at Syracuse. Make your drawing as Greek-looking as possible—the photos and drawings in Chapters 3, 4 and 5 will be a guide.

3 The pictures on page 62 show a Persian and a Greek soldier. Imagine you were a Persian soldier at Salamis, or an Athenian at Syracuse. Write a letter home explaining what happened in the battle, and how you escaped being killed yourself.

SOME BOOKS TO READ

1 Homer's *Iliad* is the story of part of the Trojan War, and his *Odyssey* tells of Odysseus's wanderings after the war was over. Virgil's *Aeneid* is the story of what happened to the Trojan survivors after the war. *The Argonauts* by Apollonios is the story of Jason and the Golden Fleece. These four books are all published complete in the 'Penguin Classics' series, and in shortened and easier form in Longman 'Heritage of Literature' series (called respectively *The Trojan War, The Odyssey of Homer, The Story of Aeneas* and *The Argonauts*.) *Odysseus Returns*, by K. McLeish (Longman Group), tells Odysseus's story as a children's novel.

2 Thukydides's *History of the Peloponnesian War* tells about the war between Athens and the other Greek states. Books VI and VII describe the expedition to Sicily and the battles there. Herodotos' *Histories*, among many other things, tell of the Persian invasions. (The battle of Salamis is in Book VIII.) Both books are in the 'Penguin Classics' series. The story of Xerxes has also been well told in a shorter form by Mary Renault in *Lion in the Gateway* (Longman, 'Heritage of Literature' series), and Rex Warner's *Athens at War* (published by The Bodley Head) tells the story of Athens's war with Sparta and her allies.

3 Books suitable for project-work are *The Ancient Mariners* (L. Casson, published by Gollancz, which is about early seafaring in many lands, not just Greece. *Ancient Crete and Mycenae* (J. Bolton, Longman 'Then and There' series) tells of the Cretans and their sea-empire. *Minoan Crete*, in the Longman 'Aspects of Greek Life' Series, also tells about Crete. *The Greeks Overseas* (J. Boardman, published by Pelican Books) is a detailed book on Greek colonies and their archaeology. *The Year of Salamis* (P. Green, published by Weidenfeld & Nicholson) is a long and detailed account of the Persian Wars. Many libraries will have these books; and those that haven't will order them for you if you ask.

SOME IMPORTANT DATES (N.B. all dates are B.C. except for the last one.)

c 2000–1400	Minoan sea-empire in Crete.
1184	Usual date given for the fall of Troy.
c 800	Homer wrote the *Iliad* and the *Odyssey*.
c 700	Hesiod wrote his book on farming.
490	Greeks defeated Persians at Marathon.
480	Greeks won the battle of Salamis.
479	Final defeat of Persians at Plataia.
c 480–425	Herodotos lived (he wrote about the Persian Wars).
c 460–400	Thukydides lived (he wrote about the war between Athens and Sparta).
431	War begins between Athens and the allies of Sparta.
415	Sicilian expedition set out from Athens.
413	Athenian fleet defeated at Syracuse.
404	Athens surrendered.
c 295–215	Apollonios lived (he wrote about Jason and the Argonauts).
c 250	Pharos of Alexandria built.
146	Greece finally conquered by the Romans.
c 625 A.D.	Invention of 'Greek Fire'.